Cambridge Young Learners
English Tests

Cambridge Starters 7

Answer Booklet

Examination papers from

University of Cambridge
ESOL Examinations:

English for Speakers of Other Languages

CAMBRIDGE
UNIVERSITY PRESS

CAMBRIDGE UNIVERSITY PRESS
Cambridge, New York, Melbourne, Madrid, Cape Town,
Singapore, São Paulo, Delhi, Mexico City

Cambridge University Press
The Edinburgh Building, Cambridge CB2 8RU, UK

www.cambridge.org
Information on this title: www.cambridge.org/9780521173698

First published 2011
Reprinted 2011
3rd printing 2013

Printed in Poland by Opolgraf

A catalogue record for this publication is available from the British Library

ISBN 978-0-521-17367-4 Student's Book
ISBN 978-0-521-17369-8 Answer Booklet
ISBN 978-0-521-17370-4 Audio CD

Cover design by David Lawton
Produced by Peter & Jan Simmonett

Contents

Introduction

The *Cambridge Young Learners English Tests* offer an elementary-level testing system (up to CEFR level A2) for learners of English between the ages of 7 and 12. The tests include 3 key levels of assessment: *Starters*, *Movers* and *Flyers*.

Starters is the lowest level in the system. Test instructions are very simple and consist only of words and structures specified in the syllabus.

The complete test lasts about 45 minutes and has the following components: Listening, Reading and Writing, and Speaking.

	length	number of parts	number of questions
Listening	approx. 20 minutes	4	20
Reading and Writing	20 minutes	5	25
Speaking	approx. 3–5 minutes	5	–

Candidates need a pen or pencil for the Reading and Writing paper, and coloured pens or pencils for the Listening paper. All answers are written on the question papers.

Listening

In general, the aim is to focus on the 'here and now' and to use language in meaningful contexts. In addition to multiple-choice and short-answer questions, candidates are asked to use coloured pencils to mark their responses to one task. There are 4 parts. Each part begins with a clear example.

part	main skill focus	input	expected response	number of questions
1	listening for words and prepositions	picture and dialogue	carry out instructions and position things correctly on a picture	5
2	listening for numbers and spelling	illustrated comprehension questions and dialogue	write numbers and names	5
3	listening for specific information of various kinds	3-option multiple-choice pictures and dialogues	tick correct box under picture	5
4	listening for words, colours and prepositions	picture and dialogue	carry out instructions; locate objects and colour correctly (range of colours is: black, blue, brown, green, grey, orange, pink, purple, red, yellow)	5

Reading and Writing

Again, the focus is on the 'here and now' and the use of language in meaningful contexts where possible. To complete the test, candidates need a single pen or pencil of any colour. There are 5 parts, each starting with a clear example.

part	main skill focus	input	expected response	number of questions
1	reading short sentences and recognising words	words, pictures and sentences	tick or cross to show if sentence is true or false	5
2	reading sentences about a picture and writing one-word answers	picture and sentences	write 'yes'/'no'	5
3	spelling of single words	pictures and sets of jumbled letters	write words	5
4	reading a text and copying words	cloze text, words and pictures	choose and copy missing words	5
5	reading questions about a picture story and writing one-word answers	story presented through 3 pictures and questions	write one-word answers to questions	5

Speaking

In the Speaking test, the candidate speaks with 1 examiner for about 4 minutes. The format of the test is explained in advance to the child in their native language, by a teacher or person familiar to them. This person then takes the child into the exam room and introduces them to the examiner.

Speaking ability is assessed according to various criteria, including comprehension, the ability to produce an appropriate response and pronunciation.

part	main skill focus	input	expected response
1	understanding and following spoken instructions	scene picture	point to the correct part of the picture
2	understanding and following spoken instructions	scene picture and 8 small object cards	place the object cards on the scene picture as directed
3	understanding and answering spoken questions	scene picture	answer questions with short answers
4	understanding and answering spoken questions	3 object cards	answer questions with short answers
5	understanding and responding to personal questions	no visual prompt	answer questions with short answers

Further information

The topics, structures, words and tasks upon which the *Cambridge Young Learners English Tests* are based are comprehensively described in the Handbook, so teachers or parents can know exactly what to expect.

Further information about the *Cambridge Young Learners English Tests* can be obtained from the Centre Exams Manager for Cambridge ESOL examinations in your area, or from:

University of Cambridge ESOL Examinations
1 Hills Road
Cambridge
CB1 2EU
United Kingdom

Telephone: +44 1223 553997
Fax: +44 1223 553621
e-mail: ESOLHelpdesk@CambridgeESOL.org
www.CambridgeESOL.org

Test 1 Answers

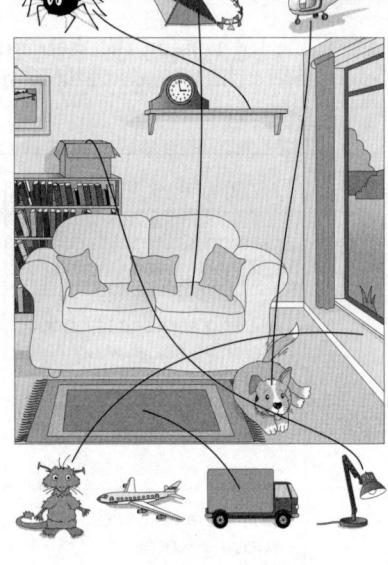

Listening

Part 1 (5 marks)

Lines should be drawn between:

1 the spider and next to the clock
2 the helicopter and between the dog's ears
3 the monster and under the window
4 the lorry and on the mat
5 the lamp and in the box

Part 2 (5 marks)

1 Alex (correct spelling)   2 14/fourteen
3 Brown (correct spelling)   4 Fruit (correct spelling)
5 18/eighteen

Part 3 (5 marks)

1 C   2 C   3 A   4 B   5 C

Part 4 (5 marks)

1 Colour the face of the frog fishing in the boat – purple
2 Colour the face of the frog with the hat, pointing to the bird – yellow
3 Colour the face of the frog with the flower – orange
4 Colour the face of the frog in the boat, with her hand in the water – pink
5 Colour the face of the frog with the ice cream – brown

TRANSCRIPT   *Hello. This is the Cambridge Starters Practice Listening Test, Test 1.*

Part 1   Look at Part 1. Now look at the picture. Listen and look. There is one example.

[pause]

WOMAN: Can you put the kite on the sofa?
MAN: Pardon?
WOMAN: The kite. Put it on the sofa.
MAN: Right.

[pause]

Can you see the line? This is an example. Now you listen and draw lines.

[pause]

1

WOMAN: Put the spider next to the clock.
MAN: Put it where?
WOMAN: Put the spider next to the clock.
MAN: OK.

[pause]

2

WOMAN: Now the helicopter. Put it between the dog's ears.
MAN: That's funny!
WOMAN: Yes! The helicopter between the dog's ears looks very funny.

[pause]

3

WOMAN: And put the monster under the window.
MAN: The monster?
WOMAN: Yes.
MAN: There. I'm putting it under the window.

[pause]

4

WOMAN: Can you put the lorry on the mat?
MAN: It's a nice big lorry.
WOMAN: Yes, it is.
MAN: Right. It's on the mat.

[pause]

5

WOMAN: Now put the lamp in the box.
MAN: Sorry? Put what in the box?
WOMAN: The lamp.
MAN: OK.

Now listen to Part 1 again.

[The recording is repeated.]

[pause]

That is the end of Part 1.

[pause]

Part 2   *Look at the picture. Listen and write a name or a number.*
There are two examples.

[pause]

MAN: Who's this?
GIRL: It's a photo of my friend. Her name's Kim.
MAN: Is that K-I-M?
GIRL: Yes.

[pause]

MAN: Has Kim got brothers and sisters?
GIRL: She's got one brother.
MAN: One?
GIRL: Yes.

Can you see the answers?
Now you listen and write a name or a number.

[pause]

1

MAN: What's Kim's brother's name?
GIRL: Alex. A-L-E-X.
MAN: Is he a nice brother?
GIRL: I don't know.

[pause]

2

MAN: How old is he?
GIRL: He's fourteen.
MAN: Fourteen?
GIRL: Yes, he is.

[pause]

3

MAN: And what's Kim's family name?
GIRL: It's Brown.
MAN: How do you spell that? Is it B-R-O-W-N?
GIRL: Yes. That's right.

[pause]

4

MAN: And does Kim go to your school?
GIRL: Yes. We go to Fruit Street School.
MAN: I don't know that school. What street?
GIRL: Fruit. F-R-U-I-T.

[pause]

5

MAN: And where does Kim live?
GIRL: She lives in the flat next to me. Number 18.
MAN: Which flat?
GIRL: Number 18. We walk to school with our mums.

Now listen to Part 2 again.

[The recording is repeated.]

[pause]

That is the end of Part 2.

[pause]

Part 3   *Look at the pictures. Listen and look.*
There is one example.

[pause]

What's Mum cleaning?

MAN: What's Mum doing?
GIRL: She's cleaning in the bathroom.
MAN: The bath or the window?
GIRL: She's cleaning the new mirror.

[pause]

Can you see the tick?
Now you listen and tick the box.

[pause]

1 What are Anna's favourite animals in the zoo?

BOY: Look at the elephants, Anna!
GIRL: Oh, yes. Are they your favourite animals?
BOY: They're OK, Anna. But I love hippos.
GIRL: My favourites are the crocodiles. They're very ugly!

[pause]

2 What's in Bill's lunch box?

GIRL: What have you got in your lunch box today, Bill?
BOY: I don't know. Let's see.
GIRL: I've got an apple and a banana.
BOY: Oh, no! I've got a carrot! I don't like them!

[pause]

3 *Which sport does Tony play at school?*

WOMAN: Which sport do you play at school, Tony? Tennis?

BOY: No, we don't have a teacher for that. We play soccer.

WOMAN: Oh, that's good. And badminton?

BOY: No, I can't play that.

[pause]

4 *Where's Grandpa?*

WOMAN: It's time for lunch. Where's Grandpa?

GIRL: He's sleeping.

WOMAN: Where? In bed or in the armchair?

GIRL: He isn't in the house. He's in the garden!

[pause]

5 *What would Nick like to do?*

MAN: What a nice beach! Let's go in the sea, Nick.

BOY: I don't like swimming.

MAN: Oh. Would you like to find shells then?

BOY: No. Let's play in the sand.

Now listen to Part 3 again.

[The recording is repeated.]

[pause]

That is the end of Part 3.

[pause]

Part 4 *Look at the picture. Listen and look. There is one example.*

[pause]

WOMAN: Look at the frog family in the park.

BOY: Yes. It's a beautiful day.

WOMAN: Find the frog in the tree.

BOY: Right.

WOMAN: Colour his face red.

BOY: OK. The frog in the tree's got a red face.

[pause]

Can you see the frog with a red face? This is an example.
Now you listen and colour.

[pause]

1

WOMAN: Can you see the boat?

BOY: Yes.

WOMAN: One frog in the boat is fishing.

BOY: Oh, yes. He's got three fish.

WOMAN: Colour his face purple.

BOY: Purple. Right.

[pause]

2

WOMAN: I like the frog with the hat.

BOY: Where?

WOMAN: He's pointing to the bird.

BOY: Oh, yes. Can I colour his face yellow?

WOMAN: Yes, colour his face yellow.

[pause]

3

BOY: There's a frog with a flower.

WOMAN: Sorry?

BOY: There's a frog with a flower.

WOMAN: Oh, yes. Colour her face orange.

BOY: Orange? OK.

[pause]

4

BOY: One frog is putting her hand in the water.

WOMAN: Oh, yes. She's in the boat too.

BOY: She's very happy. Can I colour her face pink?

WOMAN: Yes. Pink is a good colour for a face!

[pause]

5

WOMAN: Find the frog with an ice cream.

BOY: I like ice cream.

WOMAN: Me too. Colour her face brown.

BOY: A brown face? That's good.

WOMAN: Yes.

BOY: I love this picture now.

Now listen to Part 4 again.

[The recording is repeated.]

[pause]

That is the end of the Starters Practice Listening Test 1.

Reading and Writing

Part 1 (5 marks)

1 ✗   2 ✗   3 ✓   4 ✗   5 ✓

Part 2 (5 marks)

1 yes   2 yes   3 no   4 yes   5 no

Part 3 (5 marks)

1 ball 2 doll 3 robot 4 train 5 guitar

Part 4 (5 marks)

1 boy 2 chair 3 books 4 computer 5 games

Part 5 (5 marks)

1 kitchen 2 pineapple 3 children/kids 4 table
5 woman/lady/mum(my)/mother

Speaking

Part	Examiner does this:	Examiner says this:	Minimum response expected from child:	Back-up questions:
	Usher brings candidate in.	Usher to examiner: **Hello. This is (child's name*).** Examiner: **Hello, *. My name's** *Jane/Ms Smith.*	**Hello.**	
1	Points to **Scene** picture.	**Look at this. This is a garden. The boys are playing football.**		
	Points to the women in **Scene** picture.	**Here are the women. *, where's the bird? Where are the toys?**	Points to items in the picture.	**Is this the bird? Are these the toys?**
2	Points to **Object** cards.	**Now look at these. Which is the spider/lizard?**	Points to **Object** card.	**Is this the spider/lizard?** (pointing to spider/lizard)
		I'm putting the spider/ lizard next to the elephant.		
		Now you put the spider/ lizard under the tree.	Puts **Object** card in place.	**Where's the tree?** <u>Under</u> **the tree.**
		Which is the T-shirt/hat?	Points to **Object** card.	**Is this the T-shirt/hat?** (pointing to T-shirt/hat)
		Put the T-shirt/hat between the skirt and the jeans.	Puts **Object** card in place.	**Where are the skirt and the jeans?** <u>Between</u> **the skirt and the jeans.**
		Which are the glasses?	Points to **Object** card.	**Are these the glasses?** (pointing to glasses)
		Put the glasses on the mouse.	Puts **Object** card in place.	**Where's the mouse?** <u>On</u> **the mouse.**
3	Removes **Object** cards and points to an apple in **Scene** picture.	**Now, *, what's this? What colour is it? How many apples are there?**	**apple red four**	**Is it an apple? Is it yellow? Red? Are there three? Four?**
	Points to the baby.	**What's the baby doing?**	**drinking (milk)**	**Is the baby drinking?**
4	Puts **Scene** picture away and picks out three **Object** cards.			
4.1	Shows **table tennis** card.	**What's this? Do you play table tennis? What sport do you play at school?**	**table tennis yes/no** *basketball*	**Is it table tennis?** **Do you play** *basketball*?
4.2	Shows **chips** card.	**What are these? Do you eat chips/fries? What do you eat for lunch?**	**chips/fries yes/no** *rice*	**Are they chips/fries?** **Do you eat** *rice*?
4.3	Shows **giraffe** card.	**What's this? Do you like animals? What's your favourite animal?**	**giraffe yes/no** *monkey*	**Is it a giraffe?** **Do you like** *monkeys*?

* Remember to use the child's name throughout the test.

Part	Examiner does this:	Examiner says this:	Minimum response expected from child:	Back-up questions:
5	Puts away all cards.	Now, *, where do you live?	*(name of town or city)*	Do you live in *(name of town or city)*?
		What's your friend's name?	*(name of friend)*	Is your friend's name ...?
		How old is he/she?	*10*	Is he/she *ten*?
		OK, thank you, *. Goodbye.	Goodbye.	

* Remember to use the child's name throughout the test.

Test 2 Answers

Listening

Part 1 (5 marks)

Lines should be drawn between:

1 the skirt and on the crocodile
2 the sock and under the clock
3 the hat and in the hippo's hand
4 the shirt and next to the radio
5 the handbag and between the frog and the snake

Part 2 (5 marks)

1 Kim (correct spelling) 2 Sun (correct spelling)
3 15/fifteen 4 10/ten
5 Happy (correct spelling)

Part 3 (5 marks)

1 B 2 C 3 B 4 A 5 C

Part 4 (5 marks)

1 Colour the ball under the table – yellow
2 Colour the ball on the man's foot – green
3 Colour the ball next to the cupboard – purple
4 Colour the ball on the boy's T-shirt – blue
5 Colour the ball in the girl's hand – red

TRANSCRIPT *Hello. This is the Cambridge Starters Practice Listening Test, Test 2.*

Part 1 *Look at Part 1. Now look at the picture.*
Listen and look. There is one example.

[pause]

MAN: Put the jacket on the tiger.
WOMAN: Put the jacket where?
MAN: On the tiger.
WOMAN: Right.

[pause]

Can you see the line? This is an example.
Now you listen and draw lines.

[pause]

1

MAN: Can you see the crocodile?
WOMAN: Yes, I can.
MAN: Put the skirt on the crocodile.
WOMAN: The skirt? OK.

[pause]

2

MAN: Now put the sock under the clock.
WOMAN: Sorry? What can I put under the clock?
MAN: The sock.
WOMAN: Oh, yes. Right.

[pause]

3

MAN: Now find the hippo.
WOMAN: OK.
MAN: Put the hat in his hand.
WOMAN: Right. The hat is in the hippo's hand.

[pause]

4

MAN:	Now can you put the shirt next to the radio?
WOMAN:	Pardon? Where do I put the shirt?
MAN:	Next to the radio.
WOMAN:	OK. I'm doing it now.

[pause]

5

MAN:	And now put the handbag between the frog and the snake.
WOMAN:	Pardon? The handbag?
MAN:	Yes, put it between the frog and the snake.
WOMAN:	OK.

Now listen to Part 1 again.

[The recording is repeated.]

[pause]

That is the end of Part 1.

[pause]

Part 2 *Look at the picture. Listen and write a name or a number.*
There are two examples.

[pause]

WOMAN:	Hello. What's your name?
BOY:	Alex.
WOMAN:	Is that A-L-E-X?
BOY:	Yes, it is.

[pause]

WOMAN:	How old are you, Alex?
BOY:	I'm nine.
WOMAN:	Nine?
BOY:	That's right!

Can you see the answers?
Now you listen and write a name or a number.

[pause]

1

WOMAN:	Is that your friend?
BOY:	Yes, her name's Kim.
WOMAN:	How do you spell that?
BOY:	K-I-M.

[pause]

2

WOMAN:	Where does she live?
BOY:	In Sun Street.
WOMAN:	Is that S-U-N?
BOY:	Yes.
WOMAN:	That's a good name!

[pause]

3

WOMAN:	What number is her house?
BOY:	Fifteen.
WOMAN:	She lives at number fifteen?
BOY:	Yes, she does.

[pause]

4

WOMAN:	How old is she?
BOY:	She's ten now.
WOMAN:	Is she? Ten!
BOY:	Yes, it's her birthday today.

[pause]

5

WOMAN:	Does she like animals?
BOY:	Yes, she does. She's got a dog.
WOMAN:	What's its name?
BOY:	Happy.
WOMAN:	Is that H-A-P-P-Y?
BOY:	Yes, it is.

Now listen to Part 2 again.

[The recording is repeated.]

[pause]

That is the end of Part 2.

[pause]

Part 3 *Look at the pictures. Listen and look.*
There is one example.

[pause]

What's May drinking?

MAN:	What are you drinking, May? Is it milk?
GIRL:	No, I don't like milk.
MAN:	Is it pineapple juice?
GIRL:	No. I've got lemonade.

[pause]

Can you see the tick?
Now you listen and tick the box.

[pause]

1 What's Ben's favourite animal?

GIRL:	Do you like animals, Ben?
BOY:	I like monkeys.
GIRL:	Do you like lizards?
BOY:	No! They're ugly. But spiders are my favourite.

[pause]

2 What is Anna drawing?

MAN:	What are you drawing, Anna? Is it a house?
GIRL:	No! Look!
MAN:	Oh, yes, it's a car.
GIRL:	No! It's a boat in the sea.

[pause]

3 Where's Nick's mouse?

BOY: Have you seen my mouse, Mum? It's not in the box.
WOMAN: Is it on the mat?
BOY: No, it isn't. Oh, I can't find it.
WOMAN: Oh, look! It's sitting on that bookcase.

[pause]

4 What's Grandfather doing now?

BOY: Is your grandfather sleeping in the garden?
GIRL: No, he isn't.
BOY: Is he reading then?
GIRL: No. He's playing football now.

[pause]

5 Which is Sam's picture?

WOMAN: Is this your picture of a bus, Sam?
BOY: No, it's my sister's.
WOMAN: Whose is this picture of a helicopter?
BOY: It's my brother's. This is my picture – the truck.

Now listen to Part 3 again.

[The recording is repeated.]

[pause]

That is the end of Part 3.

[pause]

Part 4 *Look at the picture. Listen and look. There is one example.*

[pause]

MAN: Can you see the dog?
GIRL: Yes, he's got a ball in his mouth.
MAN: That's right. Colour that ball pink.
GIRL: Pardon?
MAN: Colour the ball in the dog's mouth pink.

[pause]

Can you see the pink ball in the dog's mouth? This is an example. Now you listen and colour.

[pause]

1

MAN: Find the table.
GIRL: Yes.
MAN: There's a ball under it. Colour it yellow.
GIRL: Yellow?
MAN: Yes, the ball under the table.

[pause]

2

MAN: Look at the man.
GIRL: Yes, there's a ball on his foot.
MAN: That's right. Colour it green.
GIRL: OK. The ball on the man's foot is green now.

[pause]

3

GIRL: Can I colour the ball next to the cupboard?
MAN: Yes.
GIRL: Is purple OK?
MAN: Yes, colour the ball next to the cupboard purple.

[pause]

4

MAN: Look at the boy.
GIRL: Yes. There's a ball on his T-shirt.
MAN: That's right. Can you colour it blue?
GIRL: OK. The ball on the boy's T-shirt is blue now.

[pause]

5

MAN: Can you see the girl? She's got a ball in her hand.
GIRL: Yes. Can I colour it red?
MAN: OK. Colour the ball in the girl's hand red.
GIRL: Right.

Now listen to Part 4 again.

[The recording is repeated.]

[pause]

That is the end of the Starters Practice Listening Test 2.

Reading and Writing

Part 1 (5 marks)

1 ✓   2 ✗   3 ✓   4 ✓   5 ✗

Part 2 (5 marks)

1 no   2 no   3 yes   4 yes   5 no

Part 3 (5 marks)

1 bike   2 robot   3 train   4 guitar   5 elephant

Part 4 (5 marks)

1 family   2 badminton   3 chair   4 birds
5 apples

Part 5 (5 marks)

1 bed   2 kitchen   3 man/father/dad(dy)
4 banana   5 floor

Speaking

Part	Examiner does this:	Examiner says this:	Minimum response expected from child:	Back-up questions:
	Usher brings candidate in.	Usher to examiner: **Hello. This is (child's name*).** Examiner: **Hello, *. My name's** *Jane/Ms Smith.*	Hello.	
1	Points to **Scene** picture.	**Look at this. This is the dining room. The girl is eating.**		
	Points to the table in **Scene** picture.	**Here's the table.** ***, where's the computer? Where are the oranges?**	Points to items in the picture.	**Is this the computer? Are these the oranges?**
2	Points to **Object** cards.	**Now look at these. Which is the lamp?**	Points to **Object** card.	**Is this the lamp?** (pointing to lamp)
		I'm putting the lamp on the desk.		
		Now you put the lamp next to the plane.	Puts **Object** card in place.	**Where's the plane?** <u>**Next**</u> **to the plane.**
		Which is the mirror/ruler?	Points to **Object** card.	**Is this the mirror/ruler?** (pointing to mirror/ruler)
		Put the mirror/ruler under the clock.	Puts **Object** card in place.	**Where's the clock?** <u>**Under**</u> **the clock.**
		Which are the carrots/ eggs?	Points to **Object** card.	**Are these the carrots/ eggs?** (pointing to carrots/eggs)
		Put the carrots/eggs on the phone.	Puts **Object** card in place.	**Where's the phone?** <u>**On**</u> **the phone.**
3	Removes **Object** cards and points to pencil in **Scene** picture.	**Now, *, what's this? What colour is it? How many pencils are there?**	pencil green five	**Is it a pencil? Is it pink? Green?** **Are there four? Five?**
	Points to the man.	**What's the man doing?**	drinking	**Is the man drinking?**
4	Puts **Scene** picture away and picks out three **Object** cards.			
4.1	Shows **grapes** card.	**What are these? Do you eat grapes? What's your favourite fruit?**	grapes yes/no *bananas*	**Are they grapes?** **Do you like** *bananas*?
4.2	Shows **radio** card.	**What's this? Do you like listening to the radio? What colour is your/this radio?**	radio yes/no *white*	**Is it a radio?** **Is your/this radio** *white*?
4.3	Shows **tennis** card.	**What's this? Do you play tennis? What do you play with your friends?**	tennis yes/no *football*	**Is it tennis?** **Do you play** *football*?

* Remember to use the child's name throughout the test.

Part	Examiner does this:	Examiner says this:	Minimum response expected from child:	Back-up questions:
5	Puts away all cards.	Now, *, how old are you?	*10*	Are you *ten*?
		How many rooms are there in your house/flat/apartment?	*6*	Are there *six* rooms in your house/flat/apartment?
		Is your bedroom big or small?	*small*	Is your bedroom *small*?
		OK, thank you, *. Goodbye.	Goodbye.	

* Remember to use the child's name throughout the test.

Test 3 Answers

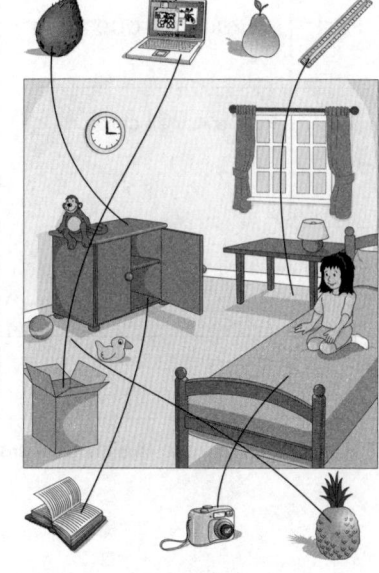

Listening

Part 1 (5 marks)

Lines should be drawn between:

1 the pineapple and between the ball and the duck
2 the ruler and under the table
3 the computer and in the box
4 the camera and on the bed
5 the coconut and next to the monkey, under the clock

Part 2 (5 marks)

1 4/four   2 Kim (correct spelling)   3 Bus (correct spelling)

4 15/fifteen   5 Alex (correct spelling)

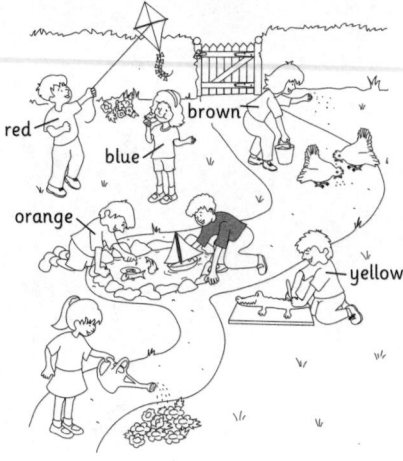

Part 3 (5 marks)

1 B   2 C   3 A   4 B   5 A

Part 4 (5 marks)

1 Colour the T-shirt of the boy looking at the fish – orange
2 Colour the T-shirt of the girl giving food to the chickens – brown
3 Colour the T-shirt of the boy with the kite – red
4 Colour the T-shirt of the boy making the crocodile – yellow
5 Colour the T-shirt of the girl eating the cake – blue

TRANSCRIPT   *Hello. This is the Cambridge Starters Practice Listening Test, Test 3.*

Part 1   *Look at Part 1. Now look at the picture. Listen and look. There is one example.*

[pause]

WOMAN: Can you see the book?
MAN: Pardon?
WOMAN: The book. Can you put it in the cupboard?
MAN: OK. It's in the cupboard.

[pause]

Can you see the line? This is an example. Now you listen and draw lines.

[pause]

1

WOMAN: Now the pineapple. Put it between the ball and the duck.
MAN: Mmm. What a nice pineapple.
WOMAN: Yes. Put it between the ball and the duck, please.
MAN: I'm putting it there now.

[pause]

2

WOMAN: And please put the ruler under the table.
MAN: Put what under the table?
WOMAN: The ruler.
MAN: Oh, OK.

[pause]

3

WOMAN: Now the computer. Put it in the box.
MAN: It's a new computer! Where do I put it?
WOMAN: In the box, please.
MAN: Right.

[pause]

4

WOMAN: And can you put the camera on the bed?
MAN: The camera?
WOMAN: Yes. Put it on the bed.
MAN: OK.

[pause]

5

WOMAN: Can you see the coconut?
MAN: Yes. Where can I put it?
WOMAN: Next to the monkey, under the clock.
MAN: All right. The coconut's next to the monkey now.

Now listen to Part 1 again.

[The recording is repeated.]

[pause]

That is the end of Part 1.

[pause]

Part 2 *Look at the picture. Listen and write a name or a number.*
There are two examples.

[pause]

WOMAN: How do you spell your name, Tony?
BOY: My name?
WOMAN: Yes.
BOY: It's T-O-N-Y.
WOMAN: Thank you.

[pause]

WOMAN: And how old are you?
BOY: I'm eleven.
WOMAN: Eleven?
BOY: Yes, that's right.

Can you see the answers? Now you listen and write a name or a number.

[pause]

1

WOMAN: Have you got a brother, Tony?
BOY: No, I haven't, but I've got four sisters.
WOMAN: Wow! That's a lot!
BOY: Yes, it is.

[pause]

2

WOMAN: And do you like your sisters?
BOY: Yes. My favourite is my baby sister, Kim.
WOMAN: Do you write that K-I-M?
BOY: Yes. She's funny. She eats her books!
WOMAN: Oh dear!

[pause]

3

WOMAN: And where does your family live?
BOY: We live in Bus Street.
WOMAN: Is that B-U-S?
BOY: Yes. My house is behind my school.

[pause]

4

WOMAN: And what's the number of your house?
BOY: It's number fifteen.
WOMAN: Sorry?
BOY: Number fifteen.
WOMAN: Oh, thanks.

[pause]

5

WOMAN: Do you like your house?
BOY: Yes. My friend lives in the house next to us.
WOMAN: What's your friend's name?
BOY: It's Alex. That's A-L-E-X.
WOMAN: That's a nice name.

Now listen to Part 2 again.

[The recording is repeated.]

[pause]

That is the end of Part 2.

[pause]

Part 3 *Look at the pictures. Listen and look. There is one example.*

[pause]

What's May giving Ben for his birthday?

WOMAN: Here you are, Ben. Happy birthday!
BOY: Thank you, May. What is it? A bus?
WOMAN: No. And it isn't a car.
BOY: Oh, it's a truck! Wow! That's great!

[pause]

Can you see the tick?
Now you listen and tick the box.

[pause]

1 Where's the soccer game?

BOY: Lucy. Come and watch the soccer with me.
GIRL: Where? On TV or in the park?
BOY: In the school hall. Our friends are playing now.
GIRL: Oh, yes! OK.

[pause]

2 What's Bill doing?

BOY: Hello, Mr Black. Can Bill come and play? Is he having breakfast?
MAN: Good morning, Tom. No, but he is here.
BOY: Is he sleeping?
MAN: I don't know. Oh, look – here he is. He's talking on his phone.

[pause]

3 Which animal is in the story today?

GIRL: Please can you read me a story, Mummy?
WOMAN: Yes. But not the tiger story again.
GIRL: OK. And I don't want the one with the goat. He's ugly!
WOMAN: I know, let's read about the happy spider!

[pause]

4 Where is Anna's pen?

GIRL: Mr White, I can't find my pen. It isn't in my bag.
MAN: Is it in your desk, Anna?
GIRL: I don't know.
MAN: I can see it. It's on the floor. Oh, Anna!

[pause]

5 Who's in the photo?

BOY: Is that your grandma or your mum in the photo, Pat? I like her long hair.
GIRL: You are funny! It's not one of them!
BOY: So who is it?
GIRL: It's my big brother! He's got long hair!

Now listen to Part 3 again.

[The recording is repeated.]

[pause]

That is the end of Part 3.

[pause]

Part 4 *Look at the picture. Listen and look. There is one example.*

[pause]

WOMAN: It's a beautiful day.
BOY: Yes. The children are playing in the garden.
WOMAN: One boy's playing with a boat. Can you colour his T-shirt green?
BOY: OK. A green T-shirt for the boy with the boat.

[pause]

Can you see the boy with a green T-shirt? This is an example. Now you listen and colour.

[pause]

1

BOY: There are some fish in the water.
WOMAN: Yes. That boy's looking at them.
BOY: Can I colour his T-shirt orange?
WOMAN: OK. The boy next to the fish can have an orange T-shirt.

[pause]

2

BOY: Look at that girl. She's giving food to the chickens.
WOMAN: That's good. Make her T-shirt brown.
BOY: OK. I'm colouring her T-shirt brown.
WOMAN: Good. The chickens are happy with their food!

[pause]

3

BOY: I like the boy with the kite.
WOMAN: Yes. Let's make that boy's T-shirt red.
BOY: OK, that's good.
WOMAN: A red T-shirt for the boy with the big kite.

[pause]

4

WOMAN: And look at that boy.
BOY: Which one?
WOMAN: The one with the crocodile. Colour his T-shirt yellow.
BOY: Is he making that crocodile?
WOMAN: Yes, he is. Give him a yellow T-shirt.
BOY: OK.

[pause]

5

WOMAN: Look. That girl's eating a cake.
BOY: Oh, yes. Can I colour her T-shirt blue?
WOMAN: Blue? Yes, OK. Would you like a cake, too?
BOY: Yes, please!
WOMAN: Come on then. Let's go and get one!
BOY: Great!

Now listen to Part 4 again.

[The recording is repeated.]

[pause]

That is the end of the Starters Practice Listening Test 3.

Reading and Writing

Part 1 (5 marks)

1 ✓   2 ✓   3 ✗   4 ✗   5 ✗

Part 2 (5 marks)

1 no   2 yes   3 yes   4 no   5 no

Part 3 (5 marks)

1 tennis   2 hockey   3 fishing   4 football
5 badminton

Part 4 (5 marks)

1 chairs   2 teacher   3 board   4 games   5 books

Part 5 (5 marks)

1 kitchen   2 man/dad(dy)/father   3 drinking
4 3/three   5 cake

Speaking

Part	Examiner does this:	Examiner says this:	Minimum response expected from child:	Back-up questions:
	Usher brings candidate in.	Usher to examiner: **Hello. This is (child's name*).** Examiner: **Hello, *. My name's** *Jane/Ms Smith.*	**Hello.**	
1	Points to **Scene** picture.	**Look at this. This is a garden. The children are getting the oranges for their mother.**		
	Points to the house in **Scene** picture.	**Here's the house. *, where's the sun? Where are the dogs?**	Points to items in the picture.	**Is this the sun? Are these the dogs?**
2	Points to **Object** cards.	**Now look at these. Which is the chair?**	Points to **Object** card.	**Is this the chair?** (pointing to chair)
		I'm putting the chair under the old man.		
		Now you put the chair on the lizard.	Puts **Object** card in place.	**Where's the lizard?** <u>On</u> the lizard.
		Which is the snake/ horse?	Points to **Object** card.	**Is this the snake/horse?** (pointing to snake/horse)
		Put the snake/horse between the woman and the cats.	Puts **Object** card in place.	**Where are the woman and the cats?** <u>Between</u> the woman and the cats.
		Which is the pineapple?	Points to **Object** card.	**Is this the pineapple?** (pointing to pineapple)
		Put the pineapple in front of the door.	Puts **Object** card in place.	**Where's the door?** <u>In front of</u> the door.
3	Removes **Object** cards and points to a bird in **Scene** card.	**Now, *, what's this? What colour is it? How many birds are there?**	**bird** **black** **three**	**Is it a bird? Is it blue? Black? Are there two? Three?**
	Points to the boy in red T-shirt.	**What's the boy doing?**	**eating**	**Is the boy eating?**
4	Puts **Scene** picture away and picks out three **Object** cards.			
4.1	Shows **phone/ television** card.	**What's this? Have you got a phone/ television?**	**phone/television** **yes/no**	**Is it a phone/television?**
		How many phones/ televisions are there in your house/flat/ apartment?	*two*	**Are there** *two* **phones/ televisions in your house/flat/apartment?**
4.2	Shows **robot** card.	**What's this? Do you play with robots? What's your favourite toy?**	**robot** **yes/no** *kite*	**Is it a robot?** **Do you like** *kites*?
4.3	Shows **rice** card.	**What's this? Do you like rice? What do you have for lunch?**	**rice** **yes/no** *chicken*	**Is it rice?** **Do you have** *chicken*?

* Remember to use the child's name throughout the test.

Part	Examiner does this:	Examiner says this:	Minimum response expected from child:	Back-up questions:
5	Puts away all cards.	Now, *, what's your friend's name?	*(name of friend)*	Is your friend's name …?
		Is your school big or small?	*big*	Is your school *big*?
		What sport do you play?	*football*	Do you play *football*?
		OK, thank you, *. Goodbye.	Goodbye.	

* Remember to use the child's name throughout the test.

STARTERS THEMATIC VOCABULARY LIST

For ease of reference, vocabulary is arranged in semantic groups or themes. Some words appear under more than one heading.

In addition to the topics, notions and concepts listed for the syllabus, the following categories appear:

- useful words and expressions
- adjectives
- determiners
- adverbs
- prepositions
- conjunctions

- pronouns
- verbs
- modals
- question words
- names

ANIMALS

animal
bird
cat
chicken
cow
crocodile
dog
duck
elephant
fish (s & pl)
frog
giraffe
goat
hippo
horse
lizard
monkey
mouse/mice
sheep (s & pl)
snake
spider
tail
tiger
zoo

THE BODY & FACE

arm
body
ear
eye
face
foot/feet
hair
hand
head
leg
mouth
nose
smile

CLOTHES

bag
clothes
dress
glasses
handbag
hat
jacket
jeans
shirt
shoe
skirt
sock
trousers
T-shirt
watch
wear

COLOURS

black
blue
brown
green
grey (or gray)
orange
pink
purple
red
white
yellow

FAMILY & FRIENDS

baby
boy
brother
child/children
cousin
dad(dy)
family
father
friend
girl
grandfather
grandma
grandmother
grandpa
live
man/men
Miss
mother
Mr
Mrs
mum(my) (US mom(my))
old
person/people
sister
their
them
they
us
we
woman/women
you
young
your

FOOD & DRINK

apple
banana
bean
bread
breakfast
burger
cake

carrot
chicken
chips (US fries)
coconut
dinner
drink (n & v)
eat
egg
fish
food
fries (UK chips)
fruit
grape
ice cream
juice
lemon
lemonade
lime
lunch
mango
meat
milk
onion
orange
pea
pear
pineapple
potato
rice
sausage
supper
tomato
water
watermelon

THE HOME

apartment
armchair
bath
bathroom
bed
bedroom
bookcase
box
camera
chair
clock
computer
cupboard
desk
dining room
doll
door
flat
floor
flower
garden
hall

house
kitchen
lamp
living room
mat
mirror
painting
phone
picture
radio
room
sleep
sofa
table
television/TV
toy
tree
wall
watch
window

NUMBERS

Cardinals: 1–20

PLACES & DIRECTIONS

behind
between
here
in
in front of
next to
on
park
shop (US store)
store (UK shop)
street
there
under
zoo

SCHOOL

alphabet
answer
ask
board
book
bookcase
class
classroom
close
colour
computer
correct
cross
cupboard
desk
door

draw(ing)
English
eraser
example
find
floor
know
learn
lesson
letter (as in alphabet)
line
listen (to)
look
name
number
open
page
part
pen
pencil
picture
playground
question
read
right (as in correct)
rubber
ruler
school
sentence
spell
stand (up)
story
teacher
tell
test (n & v)
tick (n & v)
understand
wall
window
word
write

SPORTS & LEISURE

badminton
ball
baseball
basketball
beach
bike
boat
book
bounce
camera
catch
doll
draw(ing)
drive (v)
enjoy

favourite
fish(ing)
fly
football (US soccer)
game
guitar
hit
hobby
hockey
jump
kick (v)
kite
listen (to)
paint(ing)
photo
piano
picture
play (with)
radio
read
ride (v)
run
sing
soccer (UK football)
song
sport
story
table tennis
television/TV
tennis
throw
toy
TV/television
watch

TIME

afternoon
birthday
clock
day
end
evening
morning
night
today
watch

TOYS

ball
baseball
basketball
bike
car
doll
football
game
helicopter
kite

lorry (US truck)
monster
plane
robot
toy
train
truck (UK lorry)

TRANSPORT

bike
boat
bus
car
drive (v)
fly (v)
go
helicopter
lorry (US truck)
motorbike
plane
ride (v)
run
swim
train
truck (UK lorry)
walk

WEATHER

sun

WORK

teacher

THE WORLD AROUND US

beach
sand
sea
shell
street
sun
tree
water

USEFUL WORDS & EXPRESSIONS

bye (-bye)
goodbye
hello
I don't know
no
oh
oh dear
OK
pardon
please
right

so
sorry
thank you
thanks
then
well
well done
wow
yes

ADJECTIVES

angry
beautiful
big
clean
closed
correct
dirty
double
English
favourite
funny
good
great
happy
her
his
its
long
my
new
nice
old
our
right (correct)
sad
short
small
sorry
their
ugly
young
your

DETERMINERS

a/an
a lot of
lots of
many
my
no
one
some
that
the
these
this
those

23

ADVERBS

a lot
again
here
lots
not
now
then
there
today
too
very

PREPOSITIONS

about
at
behind
between
for
from
in (prep of place)
in front of
like
next to
of
on
to
under
with

CONJUNCTIONS

and
but
or

PRONOUNS

he
her
hers
him
his
I
it
its
me
mine
one
ours
she
that
theirs
them
these
they
this
those
us
we
you
yours

VERBS

Irregular:

be
catch (a ball)
choose
come
do
draw
drink
drive
eat
find
fly
get
give
go
have
have (got)
hit
hold
know
learn
make
put
read
ride
run
say
see
sing
sit (down)
sleep
spell
stand (up)
swim
take (a photo)
tell
throw
understand
wear
write

Regular:

add
answer
ask
bounce
clean
close
colour
complete
cross
enjoy

jump
kick
learn
like
listen (to)
live
look
look at
love
open
paint
phone
pick up
play (with)
point
show
smile
start
stop
talk
test
tick
try
walk
want
watch
wave

MODALS

can/cannot/can't

QUESTION WORDS

how
how many
how old
what
where
which
who
whose

NAMES

Alex
Ann
Anna
Ben
Bill
Jill
Kim
Lucy
May
Nick
Pat
Sam
Sue
Tom
Tony